Original title:
The Search for Purpose in a Sea of Socks

Copyright © 2025 Creative Arts Management OÜ
All rights reserved.

Author: Micah Sterling
ISBN HARDBACK: 978-1-80566-081-1
ISBN PAPERBACK: 978-1-80566-376-8

Colors of Belonging

In a drawer of mismatched hues,
Colors clash and dance like ruse.
Stripes and polka dots unite,
Socks in chaos, quite a sight!

Each pair a story, slight and grand,
Lurking here at sock drawer's band.
Bright yellows sigh, and blues all weep,
Who knew belonging could be so cheap?

Threads of Meaning

In every knot, a tale is spun,
A tale of trials, not just fun.
Elastic dreams and cotton woes,
Untangle life through fabric's throes.

Each sock a thread in life's great weave,
Some fit, some flop, how can we believe?
Searching seams for wisdom's call,
But found only lint, that was my fall.

Unraveled Intentions

Tangled socks, oh where to roam?
Thoughts drift far from laundry's home.
Missing mates lie in despair,
Where's the logic in this wear?

With every load, confusion spreads,
Two turned one, like crumpled beds.
Intentions clean, but results unfold,
In sock world oddities uncontrolled.

Soles of Solitude

Two soles alone, without their friends,
Wander lonely till laundry ends.
Piled high, they plead for unity,
Yet fate remains in sock community.

Oh solitary foot, take a chance,
Join the party, start the dance!
In a world of footsies we may yearn,
For every missing mate, we learn.

The Quest for Solemates

In the drawer, I dig with glee,
Searching for a pair that's free.
Oh where's my left, what happened here?
My foot's alone, it's full of fear.

A polka dot wants to meet a stripe,
It's a tale of love, a fabric type.
But in this chaos, socks collide,
Their mismatched lives, a wild ride.

Threads of Intention

A blue sock whispers to a red,
"Join me, friend, forget the bed!"
For laundry days are quite the feast,
Of dizzy spins, we've got to feast.

The dryer's roar, a sock parade,
Each turn and tumble, new socks made.
Yet here I stand, with odd designs,
Like mismatched thoughts, in tangled lines.

Lost in the Sock Abyss

In the depths of laundry's clutch,
A sock's adventure, oh so much.
One wanders far, the other stays,
In this game, oh socks, your ways!

Perhaps a foot will take the lead,
Or maybe just a cozy bead.
The cotton dreams of pairs so grand,
But life's a mess, just as we planned.

Echoes of Unmatched Destiny

Two socks meet in a lonely pile,
"Hello," says one, with a quirky smile.
"Do you think we'll find a friend?
Let's stick together till the end!"

With tiny holes and colors bright,
Their bond grows stronger with each night.
In the mismatched world, it's clear,
Every lost sock deserves a cheer!

In Pursuit of Patterns

A sock with stripes, another with dots,
They dance on the floor in wild, tangled knots.
Lurking beneath, a lone sock in gray,
Dreaming of colors to brighten its day.

With every drawer opened, a treasure's unearthed,
Missing its mate, it feels so 'unworth'.
Yet in this chaos, a story unfolds,
Of lost laundry adventures and legends retold.

The Silent Conversation of Socks

In the corner, they whisper, those socks piled high,
A quiet debate, no reason to sigh.
One boasts of its journey, from foot to the floor,
While another just wishes to be worn once more.

Oh, how they ponder, the life they could lead,
If only their partners would answer the need.
For mismatched pairs have a tale of delight,
In their colorful world, everything feels right.

Adventure Beneath the Laundry

Beneath the basket, a wild tale lies,
Of sneakers and sandals, in socks as their spies.
They plot a great journey beyond the wash cycle,
To places unknown, oh the joy they'll recycle!

Through suds and through rinse, they swim with glee,
Each spin brings a thrill, like a rollercoaster spree.
The detour they take, a whimsical ride,
In the land of lost laundry, they joyfully glide.

The Power of Pairing

A lone sock once said, 'I'm destined for fame!'
But without its twin, it wasn't the same.
The duo at last, they happily chat,
'Together we're stronger, just look at us strut!'

Singular socks may grumble and pout,
But paired up, they shine, there's never a doubt.
In the world of footwear, they reign supreme,
Making mismatches look like a dream team!

The Muffled Echo of Soles

In a drawer so deep, they lay tucked away,
Mismatched and lonely, they dream of the day.
A flip-flop whispers to a sock in despair,
"Where's my partner? Do you think they care?"

A sandal swings by with a wink and a nod,
"You think your life's tough? Try being a clod!"
They giggle and chuckle with each little quirk,
In a world full of fabric, they find the fun work.

Knitted Dreams

A toe peeks out from a woolly embrace,
It dreams of the dance on a bright sunny face.
But stuck in a drawer, it shimmies in dread,
"Would it be better as a cozy bedspread?"

The yarn spins a tale, full of twists and of turns,
Of buttons and zippers, of laughter that churns.
With each little stitch, they plot and they scheme,
To find a new life woven into a dream.

Sewn in Search of More

A patch on a heel with a story to share,
Each leap and each bound, weaving tales in midair.
"What if I'm just lost?" a sock suddenly sighs,
"Or perhaps I'm the hero in this great disguise?"

With threads intertwined, they circle around,
In a wild sock party, where joy can be found.
One dreams of the journey, another the fun,
Who knew a mere sock could feel so undone?

Intertwined Journeys

In a basket of chaos, they frolic and play,
Adventures in laundry, they cheerfully sway.
A lone striped fellow, full of bright cheer,
"What's the story today? Who wants to steer?"

With pockets of lint, and a dance on the floor,
They waltz through the chaos—who could ask for more?
From the washer to dryer, they glide with a laugh,
Each one a companion on this wild little path.

Reverberations in Cotton

In a drawer, the chaos clings,
Lost in the folds, like forgotten kings.
Yellow, green, stripes, and polka dots,
They dance around in tangled knots.

I pull one out, it is not a pair,
A lonely sock, a soul laid bare.
I ponder what journey it might have known,
While plotting a map to its homegrown throne.

Tides of Textile

Waves of laundry, foamy and bright,
Socks scatter like stars in the night.
A green one winks, a blue one sighs,
Caught in the whirlpool of fabric lies.

The sock monster grins, a toothy glee,
As I navigate the sea of debris.
What lies beneath that soft embrace?
Perhaps the secrets of this wild place.

Where Soles Drift

In the corner, a sock begins to stray,
A journey unfolds, come what may.
Through boots and sneakers, it wanders far,
Dreaming of landing on a cozy star.

A lost toe here, a missing heel there,
Each footnote tells a life laid bare.
To find the mate, oh what a task!
While I chuckle at fate's funny mask.

Quest for the Uncommon Pair

On the floor, a questing soul roams,
Searching for company in cloth-covered homes.
Will this polka dot find its twin today?
Or will it strut in a stylish dismay?

With mismatched vibes, it marches on,
Declaring independence, and then it's gone.
Oh, the oddball charm of a solo sock,
Showing the world it's fun to rock.

An Unraveled Journey

In a drawer dim and dark,
A pile of fabric waits,
Each sock a hidden spark,
Of long-lost fates.

Pairs desired, yet always rare,
One's here, the other's gone,
A dance of colors everywhere,
A sock-based con.

The lonely ones are tales untold,
Of being ever shy,
They hide away, all tangled and rolled,
In a weave of lie.

Yet laughter echoes through the land,
As sock puppets rise,
With silly voices, values grand,
In mismatched disguise.

Finding the Forgotten

Beneath the bed, dust bunnies play,
What treasures might I find?
A lonely sock in disarray,
With memories intertwined.

Oh, the stinky tales they weave,
Adventure's scent alive,
In this land where socks believe,
That mismatches can thrive.

Some were once quite dignified,
With stripes or polka dots,
Now cast aside, they've no one to guide,
In their cozy little spots.

Yet every lost and lonely sole,
Is a hero in their right,
For deep inside each little hole,
Lies a laugh, pure delight.

Lint on the Heart

There's lint upon my heart today,
    A sock puppet's embrace,
With every twist, and every sway,
    I find a familiar face.

Each fiber holds a secret wish,
    For laughs, for fun, for cheer,
A laundry day, a mismatched dish,
    Brings memories ever near.

The holes they bear have tales to tell,
    Of journeys far and wide,
To the washer's spin, they danced so well,
    With life as their guide.

So let us cherish, never toss,
    Those pairs left all alone,
In a world that finds the humblest gloss,
    Of love so brightly shown.

The Odyssey of Unworn Footwear

A closet deep holds dreams of feet,
Yet few have dared to roam,
Those lovely heels or charms to greet,
They yearn to find a home.

Certain pairs just sit and stare,
In silence, doubt, and gloom,
While all around them, life is fair,
They linger in their room.

Each unworn shoe has traveled far,
In imagination's sway,
From beaches bright to city bazaar,
They dance the day away.

With laughter, let us free their plight,
Adorn our feet with flair,
For every pair deserves the light,
In love and life, we share.

Drowning in Cotton Dreams

In a land where socks are found,
Like tiny ships that spin around,
They sail through cycles, whirl and spin,
Lost in the froth, the quest begins.

With stripes and polka dots galore,
A mismatched crew, but still we bore,
The sea of cotton, soft and bright,
Yet where's the mate? It's out of sight.

The dryer's hum, a siren's song,
But where's the balance? It feels all wrong,
A sock adrift in sudsy foam,
Will it ever find its way back home?

Each wash a wave, each rinse a twist,
In laundry's grasp, we can't resist,
To find the mate, we dive and delve,
In piles of fabric, we save ourselves.

Quest for the Lost Pair

Adventurers in the laundry mist,
We seek the partner, we must persist,
One sock is lost, its twin is near,
But locating them brings us to tears.

Behind the machine, in a dark nook,
Lurks a sock beast, or so we took,
A worn-out mate for every sole,
But finding pairs takes quite a toll.

The quest rolls on, we trudge and laugh,
Hunting through hampers, it's quite a craft,
Through lint and fabric softener haze,
We triumph still, in our sock-filled maze.

With giggles high, and spirits bold,
We tell the tales of socks untold,
Each mismatched pair a badge of pride,
In this quirky saga, we abide.

Navigating the Laundromat of Life

A journey starts with colors bright,
Through swirling washers, take flight,
The socks collide, a dance of fate,
Who knew laundry could feel so great?

Spin cycles churn while humans wait,
With baskets full, we contemplate,
The stories woven in every thread,
And where the lost things go, we dread.

Faded blues and vibrant pinks,
In sudsy dreams, our laundry winks,
The dryer laughs as we all chase,
That sock with holes that lost its grace.

As cycles turn, we learn to smile,
Embracing chaos in laundry style,
For in the fluff, we find a way,
To play with socks, come what may.

Hidden Hues in Forgotten Drawers

Deep within the drawer's embrace,
Lies a world of socks, a cozy space,
Some are colorful, others plain,
Each lost gem, a treasure we gain.

Old buddies tucked in folded stacks,
Whispers of laundry in their cracks,
With every swipe, surprises bloom,
As unmatched shapes bring forth more room.

The quiet pairs, perfect and shy,
Greet the wanderers as they fly,
In hidden hues, a tale is spun,
Of time and warmth when lives were fun.

As we dig deep to find the pairs,
We laugh at life's little snares,
For in those drawers, we unearth gold,
With every sock, a memory told.

Tangled Aspirations

In a drawer where socks collide,
Lies a single loss, I can't abide.
Odd ones dance in colors bright,
While matching pairs are out of sight.

Elastic dreams stretch thin and frayed,
I ponder how the paths were laid.
A polka dot may chase a stripe,
Yet harmony is quite the hype.

In piles of flair, I sift and sigh,
A hunter's heart with socks awry.
Whimsical shades of blues and greens,
Compose a tale of missing scenes.

Amidst this chaos, joy I find,
Each sock a laugh, so unconfined.
With every twist and turn I see,
The fun in loss, it sets me free.

Life Among the Linens

In my closet's laundry cores,
A kingdom ruled by prints galore.
Matching's hard when they elope,
And colors spark eccentric hope.

Socks of stripes and polka dots,
Meet in corners, brew guess knots.
Daily battles with the spin,
Do I wear spots or go with thin?

Humbly tucked behind the heap,
Lies aspirations, dreams to keep.
I ponder silently, they tease,
In a circus of fabric, find my ease.

So here I stand, lost in threads,
With every step, a sock that spreads.
Amid the chaos, laughter flares,
Life among linens, fun ensnares.

Echoes of Everyday Choices

Every morning there's a scheme,
Which sock's the star of my daydream?
A colorful chaos, unmatched glee,
The best-dressed feet, oh let them be!

My laundry piles like stories told,
Lost socks whisper secrets bold.
From checkered pasts to superhero lore,
Each pattern boasts adventures galore.

Decision fatigue, a sock parade,
Should I go fancy, or beachfront laid?
Echoes linger from washing spins,
The comedy of my daily wins.

In mismatched pairs, life's delight,
With every blend, a laugh in sight.
A sock's true calling, fun ignites,
In this playful game, the heart unites.

Socking it to Searching

In every drawer, a chance to play,
Socks whisper tales in a playful way.
Each one pines for a partner's grace,
Yet here I sit, in this soft embrace.

Navigation in fabric jungles high,
To pick a mate, oh, how time flies.
Will I choose stripes or go for dots?
With only mismatched ones in my thoughts.

Socking it to the universe,
With every choice, I often curse.
Yet laughter frolics in cotton comfort,
And mismatched moments, they bring rapport.

So here I stand, a sock detective,
In a sea of threads, it's quite effective.
For in this chaos, life's a dance,
While every pair holds a hidden chance.

Patterns of the Mind

In drawers they dwell, quite a sight,
Colors and prints, oh what a delight!
What's matching? What's wrong? I can't make the call,
Socks doing a dance, I'm laughing through it all.

A polka dot pair, mysterious and bright,
While stripes stick together, in perfect delight.
They hop on the floor, like a circus gone wild,
Chasing one another like a confused child.

Missing a foot? What's the story, my friend?
Was it eaten by monsters? The tales never end!
One's off on a journey, the other's at rest,
In the game of sock life, none are truly blessed.

In this vast sea, I wander and stare,
Each sock with a tale, a life full of flair.
Whispers of cotton, their journeys not done,
In a world of odd pairs, I find joy and fun.

Soles of Silence

Beneath the bed, they quietly hide,
A rebel sock army, without any pride.
Whispers of cotton, in twilight they scheme,
Plotting their future like a wild sock dream.

A lone sock tips toes, on expedition begun,
With no destination, it's all just for fun.
The other retreats, saying, 'Stay here with me,'
But daring adventures are calling, you see!

Each drawer a fortress, a treasure within,
A parade of misfits, let the games begin!
With playful antics, they mess with my mind,
In the battle of laundry, odd pairs I find.

Giggles erupt as a pattern unfolds,
In this kingdom of fluff, absurdity molds.
For every lost soul, a sibling remains,
Together they journey through laughter and pains.

A Tangle of Aspirations

In a heap on the floor, ambition goes rogue,
Whispers of chaos in this knitted vogue.
One wants to party, another to sleep,
Among their cotton dreams, secrets they keep.

A hopeful young sock dreams of wild nights out,
While others just mope, filled with self-doubt.
They argue, they bicker, they twist, and they turn,
For in a ball of cotton, there's much to discern.

Piled in confusion, a sock-saga spins,
Of color and fabric that churns like the winds.
One lone mismatched pair defies all the rules,
In the world of the socks, it's them who are fools!

With laughter and joy, they roll on carpeted lands,
No grand scheme in mind, it's all in their hands.
As they tangle and twist, it's a riotous spree,
In this sock adventure, we all roam free.

Hidden Journeys Beneath

In the dark of the closet, forgotten they lay,
With dreams of excursions, to frolic and play.
A pair wishes set off to explore the great wide,
While a lone sock just ponders, intent to abide.

Forgotten socks yearn for the sun's warm embrace,
To waltz on the floors with the utmost grace.
One sneaks in the dryer for a spin and a swirl,
While others unite for a routine sock whirl.

The laughter erupts as they spin 'round the room,
In a whirlwind of threads, they shake off the gloom.
Searching for purpose among the lost shoes,
Together they'll conquer the confusion and blues.

Socks with a mission, to dance and to sing,
Finding their footing, oh what joy they bring!
In the chaos of patterns, through stars they'll glide,
In these hidden journeys, their spirits can't hide.

From Darkness to Dawning

In a drawer of chaos, I dig with glee,
Among the stripes and polka dots, what's for me?
A single mate from a wild fashion spree,
Lost in the abyss, who set you free?

Socks on the floor, like ships in a night,
Their colors are funky, their patterns delight.
I pair them like friends, matching left to right,
Yet somehow I wonder, is this really right?

Every sock has a story, some wild, some tame,
Worn while dancing, or stepping through rain.
I chuckle aloud, call their names with no shame,
In this cotton-clad world, they're more than just game!

So here I embark, on a journey absurd,
Through loops and through threads, life's sweetest unheard.
Embracing my follies, my laughter's assured,
In this sock-tastic saga, my heart's gently stirred.

Misplaced Moods

Oh mismatched socks, how you frolic and play,
One bright and bold, one casual gray.
Emotions like laundry, tossed in dismay,
Wrapped in the chaos of a laundry day.

The left sock is grumpy, the right one's a clown,
Together they laugh, then they both start to frown.
In a whirlpool of laughter, they spin round and round,
Searching for purpose, yet often they're drowned.

They ponder their journeys from feet to the floor,
Wishing on lint balls, for adventures in score.
With every odd pairing, they yearn for much more,
Yet find joy in mismatches, rich tales to explore!

So here's to the socks, in all their wild moods,
Together they dance, refusing to brood.
In a world of color, life's quirky interludes,
We chuckle and cheer, on our cottony cruise!

Layers of Life Left Untouched

Beneath the bed, an empire of threads,
Where left socks get lost, and right ones dread.
A kingdom of colors, where no one has led,
The layers of life, are more fun when spread.

Each sock holds a mystery, ancient and wise,
With tales of the stumbles, and unexpected highs.
They giggle as dust bunnies dance through the skies,
While role-playing heroes, in all their surprise.

In the depths of the drawer, stories await,
Of laundry mishaps, and culinary fate.
These layers of laughter, oh how they sedate,
As I shuffle through socks, emotions inflate.

So here's to our treasures, the bright and the bland,
Their layers of life, a whimsical band.
In this cotton havana, together we stand,
Laughing at socks, with joy close at hand.

Where Soles Seek Meaning

In a universe of fabric, where oddballs unite,
Soles search for meaning, though they feel slight.
Is it the stripes, or the colors so bright?
Perhaps it's the stories, that make it feel right.

With cartoon faces and patterns so loud,
These tiny companions, they stand up so proud.
In the quest for the final, a laughter-filled crowd,
They spin on their table, where sock dreams are vowed.

Puns of the foot, like threads intertwined,
All seeking a narrative, easily defined.
Yet somehow they linger, what joy they remind,
That life's in the tumble, in chaos designed.

So when we get tangled, in fabric confounds,
These soles will remind us of joy that surrounds.
In their fuzzy perspective, a truth that abounds,
That life's just a dance, without set bounds.

Underfoot Aspirations

In a drawer they slumber, tucked away tight,
Colors and patterns, a dazzling sight.
Yet here I am, with a mismatched pair,
Daring the world, with no hint of care.

Each morning I rummage, a sock hunt I face,
Finding a mate feels like a wild race.
With polka dots chasing stripes in the wind,
My footloose ambitions are finally pinned.

The Sock Odyssey

A single sock wanders, lost in the room,
It dreams of adventures beyond the gloom.
With quests for its buddy, it rolls with delight,
A sock on a mission, ready to fight.

Through laundry mountains and carpeted seas,
It searches for freedom, its mind at ease.
Along the couch, past the TV set,
A lonely existence, but no regrets yet.

Embracing the Unseen

Beneath the bed lies a kingdom untold,
Of the strangest things, both daring and bold.
Missing socks mingle with dust bunnies thick,
Forming a team for a hilarious trick.

A flip-flop convenes with an ancient shoe lace,
In a world all their own, they know just their place.
The echoes of giggles from far away lands,
A sock puppet council makes whimsical plans.

Unfolding the Unexpected

With a flick of the wrist, I toss and I turn,
Unfolding the layers, oh how they churn.
The laundry basket's a treasure trove wide,
Mysteries hidden, they must now confide.

A bright yellow sock, with a strange polka dot,
Declares a statement, 'Why not give it a shot?'
It dances and twirls as I take a deep breath,
In this world of socks, I'll never know death.

Entangled in Routine

In the drawer, they lay piled high,
Colors twirling, oh me, oh my.
Left alone, they start to chat,
Dreams of escape, where's my hat?

One is blue, and one is green,
The best of friends, or so it seems.
A traveler's quest for mismatched fame,
They giggle softly, it's all a game.

Routine pulls tight, they start to fray,
Where is the exit? They wish to play.
Sock jungle sprawling, it's quite absurd,
With swirling patterns, they're largely blurred.

In the fold, they plot their flight,
A secret mission, out of sight.
One wild leap and a joyous spin,
To find the world, where fun begins!

Reflections in a Basket

In a basket deep, they lay in mats,
Planning their escape from laundry chats.
They whisper dreams of open skies,
And dodging baskets—oh, what a prize!

Stripes and spots, an odd brigade,
Socks unite, and friendships fade.
"Who's got the scent of last week's leave?"
They all just chuckle, it's hard to grieve.

Tumbles and rolls, they spin around,
Life inside the basket—what a sound!
With each new twist, they share a laugh,
In this sock world, they're the epitaph.

But soon they'll land on the floor so bright,
And waltz away into the night.
No more dull laundry, it's time for fun,
In the sock escapade, they've already won!

Weaving Paths of Meaning

Through all the wash, the spinning's done,
A tapestry of socks just having fun.
Colors collide, creating a mess,
What story is this? Can you guess?

Each twisted yarn has tales to tell,
Of muddy footprints and winter spells.
With spin cycles, they share their fate,
From feet to floor, it's never too late.

Pattering sounds of daily wear,
Socks always have stories to share.
Unraveled dreams in the laundry drier,
Squeaky clean chaos, does it get higher?

They plot their routes, not just a pair,
Finding their way with whimsical flair.
The paths of meaning are now quite clear,
In this sock adventure, no room for fear!

Enigma of the Two

Once was a sock, bright red and bold,
With a partner gone, too much to hold.
"Where's my mate?" it cried with glee,
In squishy pockets, it longed to be free.

It sought the washer, an endless maze,
Seeking its other in vain for days.
While spinning round, it met a right,
A polka-dot friend, bringing delight.

"A match at last!" they danced with joy,
Against the odds, like girl and boy.
But then they noticed, oh what a sight,
One was heavy, and one was light!

From pairs to mismatches, they took a twirl,
The dance continued with a lively whirl.
In a world of single socks, they found a crew,
A mismatched life, but hey, fun's in the hue!

Solvent Lives

In laundry rooms, chaos reigns,
Bright socks vanish, it's such pains.
Lost in a whirl where lint resides,
One-eyed washers hold their sides.

Colors clash like clowns at play,
Matching pairs have gone astray.
A sock floats by, a lone parade,
Bright stripes and polka dots displayed.

When folding dreams become a mess,
The hidden socks, they must confess.
Whispers of cotton, tales untold,
In dark corners, secrets unfold.

They mingle, dance, in twists and turns,
As stubborn stains ignite our yearns.
Each lost sock a heart's delight,
In this wild world, we hold on tight.

Darning the Gaps

Needles flying, laughter loud,
Socks in shambles, proud they're bowed.
With thread and whimsy, we create,
Filling holes, we celebrate.

Oh, the stories, such delight,
Each patch tells of daring flight.
From kitchen spills to dog's great chase,
Hidden memories we embrace.

New patterns found, old tales patched,
Every sock singed, somehow matched.
Darning done with flair and zest,
Mismatched socks, they are the best!

In tiny stitches, love takes hold,
Of every fabric, tales retold.
Their patterns bold, in joy they dance,
In sock adventures, we find our chance.

Patterns Overlooked

In a drawer, a riot's bred,
Socks collide, nothing is spread.
Some are polka, some are stripes,
Frolicking in mismatched types.

There's a toe, and here's a heel,
Together they make quite the deal.
Searching bright colors, greens and blues,
We giggle at the crazy hues.

Falling deep in fabric fun,
Lost in patterns, laughter's spun.
A fishnet glimmer, a furry bear,
What treasures hide beneath that fare?

Crumpled dreams of mates long lost,
We twirl and spin, it's well worth the cost.
In the chaos, we find our way,
With a sock's charm, we seize the day.

Sifting Through Soles

Diving down, what do we find?
A treasure chest of colors blind.
Sifting through soles, the mismatched crew,
Ducklings, stripes, and polka dots too.

Tap dance with socks, a quirky show,
Under the bed, they twirl, they glow.
Each one whispers tales of fun,
From sunny days to rainy runs.

In every pair, a story hides,
About adventures on drifty tides.
Rubber bands and crumbs hold tight,
In this sock saga, all feels right.

So let's embrace the quirky flair,
With each odd mate, we're a daring pair.
In fabrics bright, there's joy to find,
In silly socks, we lose the grind.

Lint and Longing

In a drawer where pairs unite,
Fuzzy dreams take their flight.
Lost one here, and one went there,
Searching for a sock to wear.

With patterns bright and colors bold,
Worn-out threads, stories told.
Oh, where's the mate? What a plight!
Sock detectives in the night.

Rolling lint like cotton candy,
Socks and mysteries be quite dandy.
So many tales from toes to heel,
A mismatched life has its appeal.

Beneath the Pile

Underneath the bed it lies,
A stash of socks, a great surprise.
They conspired in the dark, it seems,
To start a cult of colorful dreams.

Stripes and dots in blissful brawl,
Missing pairs join in the call.
Craving drama, craving fun,
Hiding out till day is done.

Some are bold and some are shy,
Feeling lonely, waving bye.
Clothes, you see, do have a say,
In a game of hide and play.

Socks and Shadows

Socks find refuge in the gloom,
What secrets linger in this room?
Casting shadows on the wall,
Each a rogue with tales to sprawl.

Dancing solo, do they dare?
In soft whispers, they declare,
Lost in folds, their stories swell,
Mismatched dreams they love to tell.

Like sock ninjas on the prowl,
With little giggles, they all howl.
Plotting escapes from dryer spins,
For every loss, new fun begins.

Misfit Threads

Oh, the socks that don't belong,
Stitching tales, they sing their song.
With one so bright and one so plain,
Together they laugh through the mundane.

A polka dot with stripes ahoy,
Fashion rebels, filled with joy.
Sitting out the matching game,
They snugly join the sock parade.

Knitted hearts filled with delight,
Trading sides in morning light.
In their chaos, fun is found,
In mismatched love, so profound.

Layers of Uncertainty

In the drawer, they tumble and twist,
Colors collide, no match in sight.
Lonely socks, in pairs they insist,
Finding a mate is quite the plight.

One's polka dots, the other's stripes,
A mismatched dance on the laundry floor.
Search for a twin, oh, how it types,
Laughter rings out; who could want more?

Worn-out threads whisper tales of woe,
Each sock knows secrets, both old and new.
With every tumble, we laugh and glow,
In this chaos, joy, we pursue.

So here we stand, in sockdom's zone,
Embracing the funky, the wild, the bold.
In layers of doubts, we're never alone,
A sock's true match is worth more than gold!

Stitches of the Soul

A single sock slips behind the chest,
A long-lost friend, where could you be?
Under the bed, a tiny quest,
Stitches of laughter, oh can't you see?

The toes are frayed, the colors fade,
Yet still, they dance at the bottom of drawers.
Unraveled dreams in a laundry charade,
Funny how life can open such doors.

Oh, what a journey, this fabric trail,
Socks on adventures, the great unknown.
In every mix-up, there's a funny tale,
Sewn into life, a sock's seeds are sown.

So let's wear our mismatches with glee,
Each odd pair tells stories untold.
No less or more, just let it be,
In stitches of soul, we're brave and bold!

A Stroll through Threaded Tales

Once on a stroll through tiny threads,
I met a sock with a grand old dream.
Hop on a foot, hear what it said,
In funny colors, life ruled the scheme.

A left-foot fellow, with a right-hand smile,
They wandered through fabric, seeking their kin.
Each wobbly step made it worthwhile,
Laughter echoing, where to begin?

They danced through antics, a wild parade,
On the clothesline, they soared by grace.
Oddities cherished, never betrayed,
Time slips away, in this sock-filled space.

So here's to the socks, lost and found,
Each one a story, a joy to unfurl.
In a world of laughter, love knows no bound,
With every tread, we're bound to swirl!

Unraveled Hues

In a pile of jumbled hues,
Odd socks dance without a muse.
Polka dots and stripes collide,
Where did all the mates abide?

Colors clash with glee and cheer,
One-legged tales draw us near.
With mismatched pairs, we strut and pose,
Life's little quirks, that's how it goes.

Footprints in Fabric

Tiny footprints on the floor,
Socks retreat, then come back for more.
Chasing warmth in mismatched styles,
Laughter echoes, stretching miles.

With each print, a tale unfolds,
Of sock adventures, daring and bold.
They slip and slide, in playful glee,
Footprints left, like tales at sea.

Whispers of Worn Soles

Worn soles whisper secrets low,
Of bakery trips and winter's snow.
Each sock a memoir, a playful jest,
Where do they wander? Where do they rest?

In laundry piles, they weave their fate,
Jokes on us as we iterate.
Fold them neatly, oh what a tease,
They make us chuckle, if you please.

Beyond the Laundry Line

Hanging high, they flap and sway,
Secrets of socks in disarray.
Bold and bright, they catch the sun,
Reminders of laughter, oh what fun!

Each pair a dream, each color a song,
In this whimsical world, we belong.
So let the winds carry tales afar,
Of playful socks, our guiding star.

Weaving Whispers

In drawers deep, the socks reside,
A rainbow crew, with nowhere to hide.
They seem to giggle, they seem to cheer,
As I rummage through, with socks so near.

One striped, one polka-dot, joining the fray,
Who knew laundry could lead me astray?
With each pair lost, I ponder and muse,
A colorful conundrum, from which to choose.

They wriggle and tumble, a playful parade,
Each lost sock's tale, an adventure made.
Through washes and spins, they dance and swirl,
In this sock tango, I spin and twirl.

In Search of Solace

Among the piles, I search and I seek,
For missing mates that dared to peek.
A sock with a cat, a sock with a duck,
How did I end up with this bad luck?

Their vibrant hues call out to my eyes,
A mismatched party, a brilliant disguise.
I've got blues, I've got reds, a technicolor crew,
Yet all I desire is a matching two!

Sunsets and rainbows could learn a thing,
From this sock drama, the joy it can bring.
In a land of oddities, laughter does grow,
With each lonely sock, more stories to sew.

Twists and Turns of Destiny

In the dryer, a whirlwind, a sock carnival spins,
With twists and with turns, where the chaos begins.
Some fly high, while others get stuck,
Is it fate or just laundry? I'm fresh out of luck!

They tumble and roll, like stars in the sky,
Each journey unique, like the reasons why.
One lobby's a polka dot, the other plain grey,
In this sock saga, it's a bizarre ballet.

Navigating through fabric, I do the cha-cha,
An odd sock gala, let's all do the hora!
With no pairs in sight, yet never a bore,
In this adventure, who could ask for more?

Mismatched Melodies

In corners they hide, chaotic and free,
A symphony of colors, just waiting for me.
One's a solo, a lone little tune,
While others harmonize, with a sock-clad swoon.

Beige with a sparkle, grey with a twist,
Every mix-up's a playlist, too funky to miss!
As I dance through the laundry, the rhythm I find,
With each little sock, I leave worries behind.

So here's to the socks and their wild little fate,
In this sock-tastic ball, let's all celebrate!
A chorus of fabric, where mismatched shines bright,
In a laundry adventure, we spin through the night.

Tides of Tattered Threads

In the wash, they whirl and spin,
Lost in suds, where dreams begin.
A sock adrift, a lonely plight,
A search for mates in the fading light.

Under beds, they find their fate,
A dance of dust, oh what a state!
Pairless wonders, mismatched cheer,
A sock's life tale, we hold dear.

With polka dots and stripes galore,
Their stories told from floor to floor.
In every drawer, adventures tease,
What mysteries lie beneath the fleece?

Odd socks rally, let's unite!
A sock convention, quite the sight.
In ragged rows, they laugh and play,
Embracing chaos in their own way.

A Quest among the Quilts

Beneath the quilts, an epic tale,
Of socks that ventured, strong and frail.
With threads like maps, they scoured deep,
For warmth and comfort, dreams to keep.

They crossed the creases, valleys wide,
In search of mates, no need to hide.
Stitches whispered secrets near,
Funny journeys, soaked in cheer.

With shawls of plaid and flannel too,
"A sock for me and one for you!"
They mocked the cold with playful grace,
Finding hope in the fabric space.

And when at last, the quest was through,
The pairs rejoiced, "We always knew!"
In quilted layers, they found their place,
In joyous chaos, a warm embrace.

When Colors Collide

A splash of red on navy blue,
A brawl of hues in every queue.
Socks marching left, then flipping right,
In cotton combat, oh what a sight!

Odd colors clash like bold old friends,
Mismatched chaos, where laughter blends.
Green with stripes meets dashes bright,
In this colorful sock delight.

Patches talking, patterns bold,
Each one boasts a tale retold.
A striped brigade, a polka troop,
In this wild, woolly, sock-filled loop.

And when the laundry is all done,
The riot fades, but oh, such fun!
For every sock, a tale to tell;
In hues and quirks, we know them well.

The Fabric of Discovery

In laundry land, we seek and find,
Socks with stories, one of a kind.
A treasure hunt in shades of grey,
What adventures await today?

Each fabric speaks of wear and tear,
A pair once bold, now stripped bare.
Yet in those threads, a spark ignites,
In laughter born from playful fights.

With every wash, they twist and twirl,
In fluff and fluff, they do a whirl.
Finding purpose where none was sought,
In every crease, a little thought.

So let us cherish, every stray,
Those socks that dance in their own way.
In fabric dreams, we'll find our mark,
For every sock holds a little spark.

A Sock's Soliloquy

I tumble in the laundry's whirl,
In shades of red, and stripes that twirl.
A freedom fight with lint and grime,
Awaiting feet to call me 'prime.'

Lost in pairs, I yearn for one,
To dance beneath the morning sun.
Adventure waits in every wash,
With fragrant foes, I gleefully squosh.

Between the Stitches

In seams I dream of journeys vast,
Hitching rides on toes, a speedy blast.
I stretch my yarn, oh what a sight,
To leap from drawers, a sock's delight.

The world is vast, yet here I stay,
Tangled tales, just a twist away.
Each step I take, a new embrace,
With every wander, I find my place.

Warmth Woven in Threads

Here I am, a cozy hug,
Amidst the washer's endless tug.
My partner's lost, oh where's the mate?
I twiddle toes and contemplate.

In playful mischief, I reside,
A soft companion, here by your side.
With every wash, I hope to find,
A kindred sole, no longer blind.

Under the Pile of Potential

Here I dwell, beneath the heap,
With dreams of warmth, and light to keep.
Between the folds, a mission grows,
To find my way beneath the clothes.

A forgotten treasure in the dark,
Awaiting days to make my mark.
In silly socks, we laugh and bide,
For every footstep, there's joy inside.

The Sock Chronicles

In a drawer, a wild mess brews,
Colors clash like circus shoes.
Left with rights, I start to dread,
Where's the mate? It's back to bed.

Matching pairs are quite the myth,
I found one under the pith.
The dryer laughs, it guffaws just fine,
As I hold up this lonely twine.

Do they dance each time I wash?
In the spin cycle, are they posh?
One sock dreams of running free,
While the other's stuck in laundry's spree.

Oh, lost companions, where do you roam?
In this labyrinth, I can't call home.
Perhaps they're on an epic quest,
In sockland, I'll find the rest.

Fabricated Futures

Inside my basket, dreams are sewn,
Mysteries lie here all alone.
Worn-out borders, stripes askew,
Do I need a sock guru?

To align the rebel pairs in line,
And to make sure they all look fine.
Or is chaos part of the cloth?
Are these knots our love's true broth?

Sock singles plot and scheme about,
Dreaming foursomes while they pout.
Each a tale that begs to thrive,
In the cupboard where they contrive.

I laugh at the tales they weave,
Each tale is one I want to believe.
With each load, there's new delight,
In a world where socks take flight.

And Then There Were Solemates

Once I thought I knew their names,
But socks hide fierce little games.
One claims it's a hot affair,
While the other finds it hard to care.

They whisper sweet nothings, oh so loud,
In designs that would make me proud.
Yet one escapes, it's gone astray,
Leaving its friend to sway away.

Under the bed, a party's begun,
With misfits and clones, oh what fun!
They plan a march to sock and clog,
Underneath the lazy dog.

In fabric dreams, they seek the bliss,
Of pairs that twirl and dance like this.
These antics keep the laundry alive,
With shenanigans, they truly thrive.

Knots and Notions

Tangled threads tell tales untold,
Of sock adventures, brave and bold.
One's a knave, and the other's a sage,
They jive on fabric's well-worn stage.

Knotty notions fill my mind,
As I examine what's left behind.
Bright hues that beckon from the bin,
Where adventures of day's wash begin.

Each foot's style, a woven wish,
Socks make magic, oh let's not miss.
They pair with joy or dance alone,
In the chaos, warmth is sewn.

And as socks swing in their whirl,
I find laughter in every swirl.
To wear mismatched is quite a thrill,
In this kingdom of fluff, I'm king still.

Shadows of Threaded Dreams

In a drawer full of cotton tales,
Missing mates leave funny trails.
Bright colors dance in tangled heaps,
Where mismatched stories hide their sleeps.

Each sock a story, a destiny spun,
One bright, one dull, who had the fun?
Giggling threads weave through the night,
A sock parade till morning light.

Curled toes wrapped in liberty's bliss,
Searching through piles, I can't resist.
A purple polka dot laughs at me,
A socky life, wild and free!

So I dive to find the missing sock,
In this ocean of knitted mock.
With every dive, I grasp a fate,
On this journey, I celebrate!

Mosaic of the Misplaced

A rainbow quilt stitched from the past,
Colors blending, nothing to last.
One shoe's cousin tries to be bold,
In this mismatched world, life unfolds.

Patterns clash, yet laughter is sought,
Whimsical dreams in a tangled knot.
Finding joy in a cotton maze,
Every step a wacky craze.

Searching high, searching low,
Where'd that other one go?
Socks with stripes, or a sock with flair,
Connected by love, that's what we share!

Lost treasures wrapped in fabric seams,
Swirling about in frayed-up dreams.
Here's to socks that dare to be free,
A jolly dance in sock jubilee!

Navigating a Footwear Labyrinth

In the depths of the laundry's dark mist,
Lurks the twin of a sock I've missed.
Round and round in circles I prance,
Hoping to find that fateful romance.

Can they hide in the dryer's embrace?
Soft cotton whispers in this strange place.
I tumble and roll through layers of linen,
In this maze of fabric, oh, what a spin!

Spaghetti socks and noodle ties,
Twisted together, an epic size.
Each pair a puzzle, a quirky cheer,
In this labyrinth, joy feels near.

With each stumble, I giggle with glee,
For every lost sock is a victory.
Festivities born from tangled despair,
On this journey, it's laughter we share!

Fabricated Dreams

From the dryer's belly, sock chaos reigns,
Bright mysteries woven in threads and chains.
Twirling around in a dance so grand,
Every single sock wants a hand!

Poking my head through the fabric void,
Searching for pairs I can't avoid.
A polka-dotted wonder gives me a wink,
As I pause and finally think.

Each stitch a memory, spinning around,
In this universe, chaos can be found.
Socks with stories all have a charm,
Wrapped in laughter, they mean no harm.

So here I stand, in the fabric glow,
Embracing the chaos, a colorful show.
With every mismatched moment I see,
Life's just a sock party, wild and free!

Footprints in Fabric

Amidst a heap of wools and blends,
I wander lost, where do they end?
A lonely sock rolls with a sigh,
Its partner's gone, oh my, oh my!

I kneel to search, but find a dream,
Of mismatched lives, not what they seem.
One striped, one polka, a quirky duo,
Stitching together a vibrant tableau.

The dryer swallows, it plays a game,
With socks that vanish, never the same.
Each time I peek, a new surprise,
Is that a foot or a sock disguise?

In the chaos, I laugh and muse,
Fabric tales, oddities to choose.
A life of color, so wild and free,
Who knew socks could bring such glee?

Match the Unmatched

In my drawer, a carnival waits,
Of socks with stories, odd little mates.
Where is the pair of this bright one?
A journey begins, here comes the fun!

One polka dot, one stripey bliss,
How could I ever let them miss?
They dance alone, each on their quest,
To find their match, oh what a jest!

The odds are stacked, a maze of threads,
A challenge found where laundry treads.
With each oddball, a grin I bear,
In mismatched socks, I'll strut with flair.

They lost their way, those wooly pals,
Yet here they are, a party of gals!
In my heart, they're all the same,
No need for pairs in this sock game!

Patterns of Possibility

A kaleidoscope of shapes and hues,
Each little sock, a path to choose.
I jive through patterns that make me grin,
The world is bright where socks begin.

The dashed and dotted, the bold and spry,
Who says a sock can't reach for the sky?
With every step, a story breaks,
In knitted comfort, my spirit wakes.

From argyle dreams to stripes that shout,
Every sock has something to tout.
They teach me well, in silly ways,
To find joy in the fabric's maze.

In each "lost" sock, a chance to see,
That mismatched feels like being free.
So here I stand, with socks that cheer,
In this fabric dance, there's nothing to fear.

Footnotes in Life's Journey

As I step, I leave my trace,
In the laundry's wild spinning race.
Footnotes scribbled in thread and seam,
Life's a sock drawer, a whimsical dream.

One foot in plaid, the other in lace,
Every mismatch has its own place.
Twists and turns in fabric lore,
Each lost sock opens a new door.

I roam the lands of cotton and wool,
In a sea of colors, oh so full.
Who knew that socks could teach so much?
A comedy of fabric, a gentle touch.

So let's embrace these playful styles,
In our mismatching, live with smiles.
For in every pair, and in every cheer,
Socks remind us, the fun is near!

In the Depths of the Drawer

In a drawer where shadows play,
Socks lie stacked in bright array.
Some are striped and some are polka,
Lost their mates, like socks from Vulcan.

I've searched through red and purple too,
Hoping for a match, just one or two.
But they giggle in their cotton bliss,
Mocking me with every miss.

Beneath a lonely winter glove,
A treasure trove that I once loved.
I wonder if they plot and scheme,
To hide from me, or so it seems.

Yet still I rummage, day by day,
In hopes a pair will see the light of day.
For every twist and every turn,
More lonely socks I gladly earn.

Orphans of the Wardrobe

In the wardrobe, a sad parade,
Of little socks that fate betrayed.
One's a punk, the other's plain,
Together they'd make quite a gain.

They share their tales of missing kin,
Each worn thread, a tale within.
Whispers echo, oh woe is me,
Where's my mate? Oh sock, set me free!

With colors bright and textures rare,
They plan escapes from fabric lairs.
What's a sock to do but dream,
Of runner days and friendship's beam?

Through piles of duds and tangled fate,
These orphans hope for life, not fate.
And in the scrimmage, they'll unite,
For hand-me-downs can feel just right.

The Odyssey of the Left Sock

There's a left sock that seeks the right,
On a journey both strange and light.
With every hop, it skips and bounds,
Avoiding the traps of laundry mounds.

It dodges lint and twists of fate,
To find a match, oh would it wait!
Up on the dryer, down in the wash,
Its quest is grand, like Greek mythosh.

Through the land of the unmatched,
It navigates the great unlatched.
It dreams and schemes, a silly plot,
To find its friend, oh silly sock!

Yet who would think such a thing so grand,
A single sock, in a lonely land?
A hero's quest for fabric mate,
It's just too funny - don't hesitate!

Casting Lines to the Mundane

With rods and reels of everyday,
I fish for socks that went astray.
In waters deep and tubey blue,
Each cast a hope, a match anew.

I bait the hook with colorful threads,
While other laundry perches, spreads.
The mundane twists and turns just right,
Caught in a whirl, all socks take flight.

Oh what a catch, a pattern rare,
A speckled pair! Oh do I dare?
To reel them in with laughter wide,
As they flop and flounder, side by side.

Yet in this game of cotton chance,
I dance with mismatched socks in trance.
The mundane turns to joy, behold!
In socks, dear friend, true tales unfold.

Faded Threads of Fate

In the drawer, chaos reigns,
Odd socks smiling, full of stains.
One's striped, the other polka-dot,
Could these be the clues I've sought?

Lost in fluff, I stumble deep,
Among the fibers, secrets keep.
Each pair a story, each thread a dream,
Am I lost, or do I scheme?

Tumbling through the laundry dance,
What's my goal? To find romance?
Or perhaps to discover style,
With mismatched flair that makes you smile?

Beneath the bed, they dive and hide,
In forgotten realms, they take a ride.
A journey of fabric, threads entwined,
Faded friendships, socks in kind.

The Thread that Connects

A sock emerges, bright and bold,
While its sibling feels so old.
Together they search, side by side,
Through tangled paths, they giggle wide.

Lost in the sock sea, what a sight,
Waves of colors, a vibrant plight.
Can one sock find its soulmate here?
With every fold, it conquers fear.

With a wink and sparkle, they unite,
Dancing on feet, feeling just right.
But oh, the tales they have to share,
Of wild adventures, everywhere!

In every wash, they frolic free,
Bonded by fluff, just you and me.
Each wash and tumble, a brand-new chance,
To kick up fun and sock it up in dance!

Strides of Self-Discovery

One single sock on the journey of life,
Hopes to escape the mundane strife.
Beneath the bed, it's rather bold,
With dreams of adventures yet untold.

Through each wash, the courage grows,
Like tiny feet dancing on their toes.
A sprinkle of laughter, a twist of fate,
Each thread a story, oh, isn't it great?

They ponder on being lost or found,
When tossed about, spinning round.
Do they care for style or comfort sway?
In the land of socks, it's all a play!

With every step, they find their voice,
In colorful chaos, they rejoice.
Every sock a traveler, spirits flight,
In the realm of fabrics, shining bright.

Socks in the Wind

Once two socks flew high and free,
Dancing together, what glee to see!
They flapped with joy in gusty air,
Creating trouble without a care.

"Oh look! A dryer! Let's take a spin!"
They twirled and twisted, a wild grin.
With every breeze, they soared and spun,
Two funky friends, just having fun.

They fluttered through the laundry line,
Entangled in dreams, feeling divine.
And as they floated, what could it mean?
In a world of fluff, they ruled the scene!

With giggles and laughter, they found their way,
In fields of socks, they loved to play.
The wind may toss them, but do they mind?
In a socky adventure, the joy they find!

Close Encounters with Fabric

In the drawer, a wild shock,
One lonely sock begins to talk.
"Where's my mate?" it starts to plea,
"Perhaps lost in laundry's sea!"

A polka dot sock and striped friend,
Debating where this chaos will end.
Beneath the bed, they start a quest,
Wading through creases, they jest and jest.

Encounters with lint and crumbs galore,
They laugh at the socks that came before.
Through toes and heels, they weave their fate,
A mismatched pair, but oh so great!

So if you find that single sock,
Don't fret, it's on a comical walk.
Next time you're folding all your clothes,
Remember the journeys that fabric knows!

Soles and Souls

In the land where all socks roam,
A sole sits lonely, far from home.
"Where's my twin?" it cries out, loud,
In a sock drawer, oh so proud.

A dirty sock just gives a grin,
"Who needs a pair to make a win?"
With holes and stains, it wears with flair,
Says, "I'm a rebel, I simply dare!"

Toe to toe, they dance with glee,
No matching sets, just wild and free.
In mismatched pairs, they find their bliss,
In each sock's heart, a quirky kiss.

So here's to soles, and souls too bright,
Living vibrant in morning light.
In chaos, they find their ultimate track,
No need for a partner, just never look back!

Seeking Sanctuary in Stitches

Deep in the corner, beneath a mound,
A colorful sock is nowhere found.
Through threads and seams, the tales unfold,
Of adventures stitched in colors bold.

In tangled nests with yarns so fine,
A toe-eyed treasure seeks a line.
"Can someone rescue me from this heap?"
With giggles, the fabric begins to peep.

Amidst those threads, they share their tales,
Of dirtied days and mishaps that fail.
In every stitch, a memory grows,
From laundry wars to playful throws.

With wobbly edges and buttons too,
Their sanctuary's built with laughter anew.
So here's to fabrics that dream and weave,
In a patchwork world where they believe!

Chronicles of Careworn Fabric

Oh, the chronicles of fabric worn,
Where faded dreams and stains are born.
In the attic high, tales whisper low,
Of lost adventures from long ago.

A weary sock with holes galore,
Proclaims, "I've traveled, oh so much more!"
Through puddles, mud, and days so bright,
Lived life with zeal, in day and night.

With each little tear, a story to tell,
Of cozy feet that rang the bell.
From warm summer nights to chilly falls,
These threads hold secrets of countless calls.

So gather 'round for a tale to spin,
Of socks with heart and little to win.
In every fold, a journey sprawls,
In careworn fabric, true magic calls!

www.ingramcontent.com/pod-product-compliance
Lightning Source LLC
Chambersburg PA
CBHW051658160426
43209CB00004B/943